Sentimental Journey

SEQUEL

Gwen Graffenreed

To order additional copies of this book, contact:
Xlibris
1-888-795-4274
www.Xlibris.com
Orders@Xlibris.com

ISBN: Softcover   978-1-4415-4114-7
         EBook   978-1-9845-8724-4

Print information available on the last page

Rev. date: 06/27/2020

Dedication

To my Great–great Aunt Annie, mother Rebecca
and other family members who influenced my life
by instilling strong family ties, love and cultural pride.

Sacred Heart Roman Catholic Church
Greenville, Mississippi

St. Barbara Catholic Church
St. Louis, Missouri

Our Lady of Peace Catholic Church
Cleveland, Ohio

National Mental Health Organizations

Historical Events

One hundred year old family lithograph of Presidents and Cashiers of the Negro Banks of Mississippi dated 1909 owned by Annie Reed-Pope survived the 1927 Mississippi floods.

Dr. Martin Luther King Jr. and countless other brave Americans fought and sacrificed their young lives for human and civil rights. Their movements paved the road for Barack Obama's journey to the White House.

Barack Obama, the son a Kenyan Scholar and an Anglo–American mother is the first person of African descent to win the 2009 presidency of the United States of America.

Barack Hussein Obama is the 44th President of the United States of America. Michelle Obama is now the first African American woman to serve in the role of the first lady.

This book is written primarily to share information of how a southern family survived the worst flood in history and instilled cultural pride through a series of family photographs, lithographs, strengths, values and a sense of family pride which are all more valuable than dollars and cents.

Great–great Aunt Annie was a remarkable woman of excellent character. She began her journey in Mississippi around the 1870's and lived the majority of her life in Greenville, Mississippi. Greenville is located in the heart of the Mississippi delta and considered by some to have some of the richest agricultural land on earth.

She married into the Pope family and became very involved in her community. She was somewhat of a "Socialite" associating herself with the elite. She made her quiet mark in her community as a school teacher. She also kept very active in her community affairs. Her life exhibited the strengths of multicultural families through out the years - strong kinship bonds, adaptability in family roles, strong work ethics, strong religious beliefs and strong emphasis on educational achievement.

Great-great Aunt Annie Reed - Pope

When her brother Burl and sister–in–law both passed away at early ages, Aunt Annie undertook the awesome responsibility of mothering their four children Annie Lee, Burl Jr., Lucious and Will. She raised her niece and nephews quite well teaching them to be well mannered and industrious. She knew they would not survive if they were just average or mediocre.

She believed that they had to have an education that would equip them to excel, so she enrolled them in Catholic School. With her guidance these children grew up to become productive members of the community. Annie Lee was a homemaker, Burl Jr. became an elevator operator, Will, a well dressed gentleman, worked in a grocery store performing many duties and Lucious became a presser in a laundry. They owned property in and around Greenville, Mississippi.

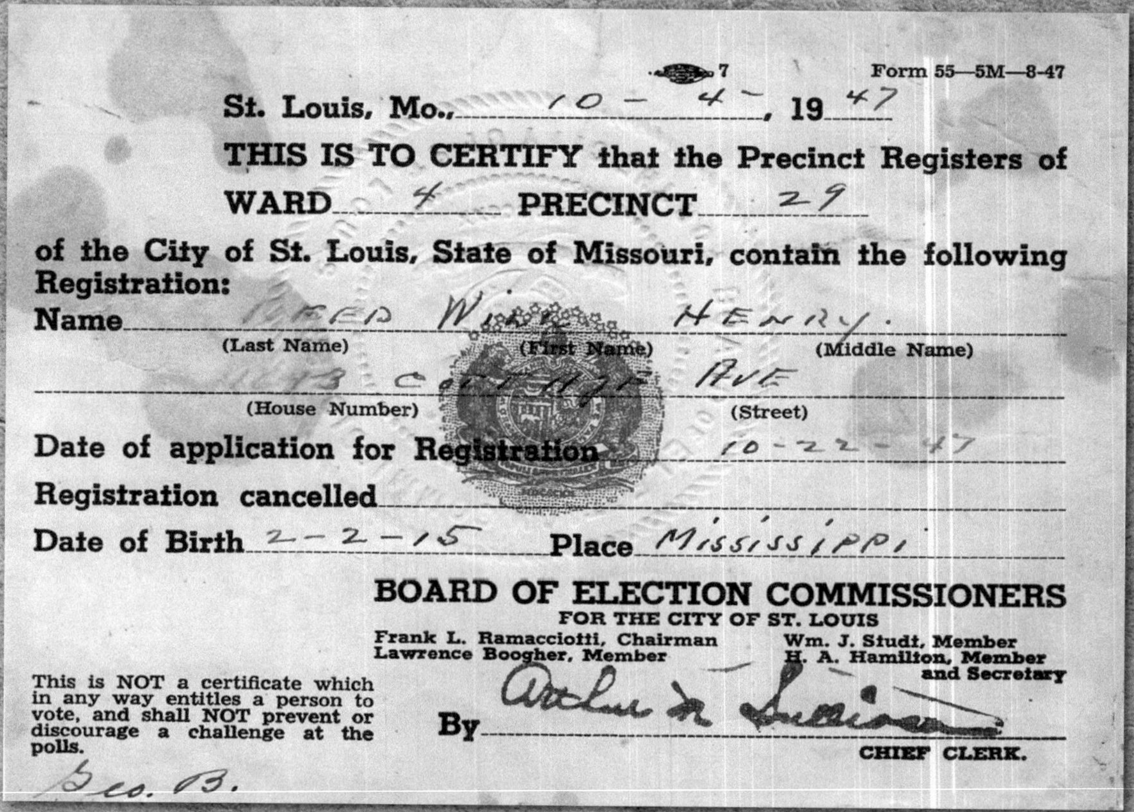

Form 55—5M—8-47

St. Louis, Mo., 10 - 4 -, 1947

THIS IS TO CERTIFY that the Precinct Registers of

WARD 4 PRECINCT 29

of the City of St. Louis, State of Missouri, contain the following Registration:

Name REED Will HENRY.
(Last Name) (First Name) (Middle Name)

43 Cottage Ave
(House Number) (Street)

Date of application for Registration 10-22-47

Registration cancelled

Date of Birth 2-2-15 Place Mississippi

BOARD OF ELECTION COMMISSIONERS
FOR THE CITY OF ST. LOUIS
Frank L. Ramacciotti, Chairman
Lawrence Boogher, Member
Wm. J. Studt, Member
H. A. Hamilton, Member and Secretary

This is NOT a certificate which in any way entitles a person to vote, and shall NOT prevent or discourage a challenge at the polls.

By Arthur ... Sullivan
CHIEF CLERK.

Geo. B.

Board of Election Registration
Will Reed 1947

Uncle Will and Aunt Katherine's
Wedding Breakfast Party
1958

She enjoyed reading, cooking, sewing, gardening, fishing and entertaining in her well kept home, which she enjoyed decorating with various pieces of art as well as with family photographs and photo collage of twenty–one Presidents and Cashiers of the Negro Banks of Mississippi dated 1909.

In 1927, the United States experienced the worst flood in history. It was the winter of 1926–1927 that rain fell so heavily throughout the entire Mississippi valley. It covered the states of Missouri, Illinois Arkansas and Mississippi. The Mississippi River and tributaries in all these states swelled and overflowed. Levees broke, causing floods in Oklahoma, Kansas, Illinois and Kentucky as well. Lives were lost and property destroyed. One writer documented that there was "more water, more damage, more fear, more misery and more deaths by drowning than any American had seen before". And yet, mysteriously or miraculously Aunt Annie's lithograph survived with only a little water damage.

One of Aunt Annie's family treasures, her lithograph of Presidents and Cashiers of the Negro Banks of Mississippi dated 1909 survived the 1927 Mississippi floods. In the photograph there is one woman cashier Mabel Z. Mollinson and her husband W.E. Mollinson, President of Lincoln Savings Bank in Vicksburg, Mississippi. Their capital was listed as $25,000 when incorporated in 1902.

It is encased in a beautiful carved frame, which shows water stains from which it survived with only little water damage. It remains in good condition today in its original carved wood frame.

*Lithograph of Presidents and Cashiers
of the Negro Banks of Mississippi*

We don't know exactly how it survived, or was retrieved from devastation. Perhaps it was because Aunt Annie's home had higher elevation. Nor do we know the reason this particular piece became a sentimental treasure of the REED–POPE, CONVINGTON family. Perhaps one of the Negro Bankers Presidents or Cashiers was a family member or someone deeply loved by the family. Suffice to say that through some divine intervention it survived such a monumental devastation as the flood. Maybe this simple fact is the reason it became so precious to those family members who passed it on and is now taking me on a sentimental journey.

The Negro Banks of Mississippi

Nineteen Hundreds

The Southern Bank

Lincoln Savings Bank

Bank of Mound Bayou

Delta Penny Savings Bank, Greenville

American Trust and Savings Bank

Bluff City Savings Bank

Delta Penny Savings Bank, Indianola

Magic City Bank

Union Savings Bank

Peoples Penny Savings Bank

Penny Savings Bank

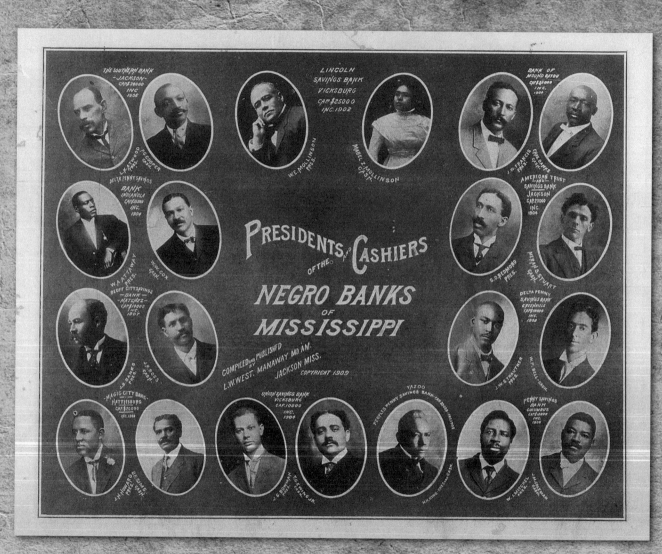

Lithograph of Presidents and Cashiers
of the Negro Banks of Mississippi

Aunt Annie had a membership with the financial institution Delta Penny Savings Bank in Greenville, Mississippi that was organized in the year of 1907 with a capital of $25,000. John W. Strauther was the bank President at that time.

He would do any kind of work as long as it was respectful to him and his community. He struggled and held a variety of occupations and saved his money. He was in the grocery and funeral business. He held a position as secretary of the Union Guaranty Insurance Company of Mississippi and President and manager of the Queen City Realty Company of Mississippi.

He truly was a business man who owned a lot of property in Greenville, Mississippi. The John W. Strauther office building was located on a well known business street in the city.

John W. Strauther

Photographs That Survived The Mississippi 1927 Floods

*Photographs tell the story
of our ancestors' successes,
and struggles*

Rebecca Convington–Reed
Great Grandmother

Rebecca Reed
Baby Photograph

Photographs of the family
1927 – 1950's

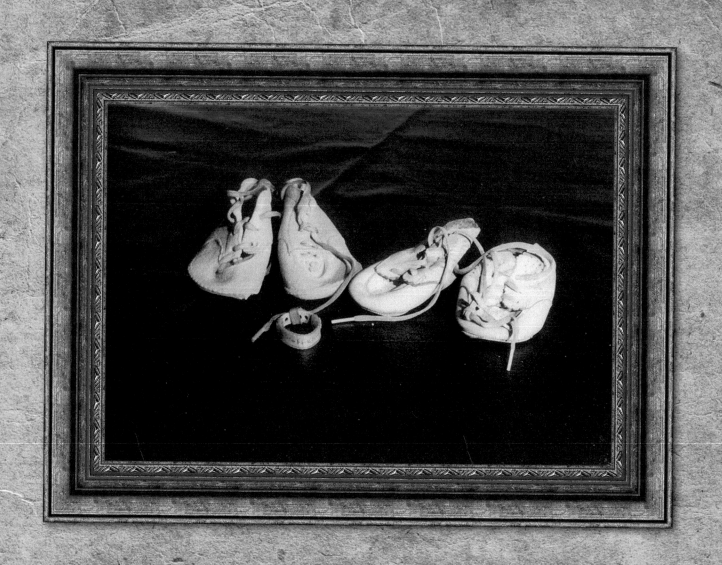

Gwen Graffenreed's
Baby Shoes

Grandfather Lee

Mamie Brown–Goodwin
Great Grandmother

Reuben Convington
Great–great Uncle

Aunt Arnetta Sneed
1949

Ed Goodwin
Great Uncle

1955 Funeral
Maggie Goodwin Graffenreed
Grandmother

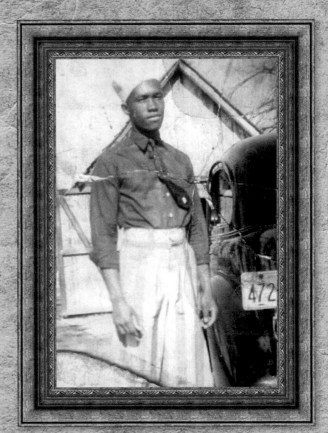

Rebecca and Clifton
Mother and Father

Cousin Katherine

Cousin Roger
1927

Aunt Katherine Sneed's
Social Club Members

Aunt Katherine Sneed's
Social Club Members

Printed in the United States
By Bookmasters